DEATH

DEATH

BY LYDIA ANDERSON

Franklin Watts
New York/London/Toronto/Sydney/1980
A First Book

FRONTISPIECE: IN THIS GREEK CARVING
FROM THE SIXTH CENTURY B.C.
A DYING WOMAN IS COMFORTED AS
HER HUSBAND GRIEVES.

Photographs courtesy of:

The New York Public Library Picture Collection:
opp. title page, pp. 41, 56, 61;
United Press International: pp. 11, 48;
National Library of Medicine: p. 20;
The First Congregational Church, Old Greenwich, Conn.: p. 34.

Library of Congress Cataloging in Publication Data

Anderson, Lydia.
Death.

(A First book)
Bibliography: p.
Includes index.

SUMMARY: Discusses the cycle of life and death,
burial customs of the past and present day,
and grief and mourning.

1. Death—Juvenile literature.
[1. Death] I. Title.
HQ1073.A52   155.9'37   79-23683
ISBN 0-531-04107-7

CONTENTS

With love and admiration,
I dedicate this book
to my mother's memory

LEARNING ABOUT DEATH

As long as people have lived, they have wondered about death. We wonder about death, too. What is it? What does it mean?

Why does a strong, healthy person grow old, or get sick, become weak, and die? What causes illness and disease? How does it feel to die? And what happens after death? Do the dead live on in another world? Or do they come back in a different form to the world of the living?

We know the answers to many of these questions. But we don't know them all. In some ways, death remains a mystery. And we are often afraid of things we do not fully understand.

Thinking about any new and unknown experience—like moving to a new town or going to a new school—*can* be frightening. Especially when no one has been there and come back to tell us what it is like. The thought of leaving everything we know in life and going into the unknown experience of death can be particularly frightening.

And, even though we often understand the cause of death, we are sad when death comes close to us. We are hurt and unhappy when a pet animal, a friend or neighbor, or relative dies. The death of another may frighten us, too, because we fear it could happen to us. Sometimes we even have feelings of guilt, as if we were somehow to blame.

Learning more about death and dying helps us to deal with these feelings. And, as death becomes less of a mystery to us, we will begin to understand that it is a natural and necessary experience in the life of every living thing.

MYTH AND SUPERSTITION

At some point, probably very early in the development of human life, human beings learned that sooner or later everyone dies. In prehistoric times, when most people died before they reached the age of 20, violent death was common. People were killed by wild animals and the clubs of enemies or by floods and fires and storms they could not control or protect themselves from.

They grew to understand the causes of violent death. But, death from "natural" causes—the wearing down of the body through illness, disease, or aging—puzzled them.

In those primitive days, there were no doctors or scientists to explain how sickness and aging change our bodies and what causes death. Like thunder and lightning, the movement of the stars and planets, the rise and fall of the tides, and other natural occurrences, death was a mystery.

And, because death was a mystery, people feared it. To make it less frightening, they invented myths and superstitions to explain death in terms they could understand. Primitive people still do this today.

The Romans thought that thunder and lightning were the weapons of their great god Jupiter. Other ancient people thought they were signs that the gods were angry, roaring and flashing their displeasure to the people of the earth.

With the same kind of reasoning, people long ago believed death was caused by evil spirits dwelling in the body. Or, that gods, magicians, or sorcerers brought it about. In India, they once thought death was the punishment of an angry god for breaking a *taboo*—an act forbidden by religious or tribal custom. Primitive people believed that magicians working for their enemies brought on death.

Even today, followers of the cult of *voodoo*, on the island of Haiti in the West Indies, believe that a witch doctor can cause death by making an image of a person and sticking it with pins. Some primitive tribes put the image of an enemy in a canoe and set it adrift, or make an image of wax and melt it over fire.

Australian aborigines practice magical bone-pointing: a priest, or *shaman*, chanting magic spells and curses, points a sharply whittled bone or sliver of wood toward an enemy. The shaman's power is supposed to turn the bone into an invisible dart which pierces the heart of the victim, causing death.

UNDERSTANDING DEATH

Today, we know that such superstitions are not true. Science teaches us that lightning is a flow of electricity formed high above the earth, and that thunder occurs when air expands after being heated by lightning. Understanding an electrical storm helps us to fear it less and to take proper measures when one strikes.

Understanding death helps us to fear it less, too.

But, in our society, death is often considered a forbidden subject and is either hidden or ignored.

Americans, in particular, have put such an emphasis on being young and staying young that aging and dying have become looked upon more as signs of failure rather than as natural stages of life. Only in the past few years have we begun to bring death into the open and freely discuss our feelings about it.

Human beings live most of their lives with the knowledge that their own death will someday come. Coming to terms with death is part of being human.

THE CYCLE
OF LIFE

To everything there is a season . . . :
A time to be born and a time to die.

Ecclesiastes 3:1–2

There are over 4 billion people in the world. Over 50 million of them die in a year. Everyday, about 360,000 people are born and about 145,000 people die. In 1978, in the United States, 3,329,000 people were born and 1,924,000 died. Birth begins the *cycle,* or pattern, of life, and death completes it.

Every living thing has a natural cycle—a series of stages through which it passes during its lifetime: birth, growth to *maturity* or *adulthood,* reproduction, aging, and death. Each stage is an experience, a passage to the next experience. Death is the final one.

The simplest forms of life are one-celled animals and plants that reproduce by dividing themselves into two or more cells. In place of death, a sort of disappearing act occurs. In the process of *fission,* or splitting, the original form ceases to exist. But life continues. And the original cell lives on in the surviving cells.

PLANTS

There are about 350,000 species in the plant kingdom. The plants we know best are the seed-bearing plants including grasses and vegetables, trees and flowers.

In the spring, we sow a bean seed in the garden. Soon, roots develop and a plant sprouts. Nourished by the sun and earth, the plant grows and forms buds. It blossoms and produces flowers and fruit—the beans we cook and eat for supper. It also bears the seed of a new plant. Then, when fall comes, it fades and dies.

The length of time between the birth and death of a living thing is called its *life span*. The life span of a bean plant, or a petunia, is one summer. An oak tree has a life span of two or three hundred years. A bean or a petunia has one seed-bearing season. The oak has many years of reproductive life. So do many other plants that reproduce in different ways.

Plants that are weak or diseased die and make room for healthier plants. If some bean plants did not die, there would soon be too little living space for fresh new bean plants. We sometimes help nature by "thinning out" the plants that grow in our vegetable gardens.

Plants sprout, bear seeds, and die. A new plant sprouts.

The remains of a dead plant *decompose,* or break down, in the earth and help produce food for plants and animals to come. The seed brought into existence by the dead plant gives life to a new plant. The seed contains directions for the new plant which enable it to carry on, or *perpetuate,* the species to which it belongs.

Each new living thing is, in some way, the product of what has gone before. The rhythm of nature flows on. Life renews itself again and again.

ANIMALS

In the animal kingdom, life begins as a fertilized egg. Different animals, like different plants, have different life spans and individual life cycles take many forms. But, the pattern of development is the same: birth, growth and maturity, reproduction, aging, and death.

A species of *rotifer,* a tiny fresh water animal, is born, grows into an adult in less than one week, lays its eggs in the next week, ages for another week, then dies.

Some insects, like the mayfly, live for only a few hours; some for weeks or years. The adult mayfly usually lives for a single day. The locust (or cicada) has a strange life cycle. It grows for seventeen years, then reproduces, ages, and dies in one! The butterfly takes four different forms during its life cycle, beginning life as an egg; changing to a caterpillar; then to a *chrysalis,* or *pupa;* and, finally, to an adult butterfly. Life as an adult butterfly lasts from a few weeks to a year.

Frogs begin life as water-breathing tadpoles. When they become adults, they lose their tails, grow legs, and breathe air.

A baby bird develops inside an egg in a nest. A sparrow hatches in about twelve days (other birds, in eleven to eighty days). Soon its eyes open, its feathers grow, and it is ready to make its first flight. When it becomes an adult, and the mating season approaches, a new nest is built. The female lays her eggs and a new life begins. Some maximum life spans include: four years for a blue jay; seven for a chickadee; twelve for a robin; twenty-four for a canary.

It takes twenty years for an elephant to reach its full growth. Signs of old age begin to appear at 40. The maximum life span is about 60.

Few animals, other than pets, reach their full life span. Some of them are killed by other animals. Others die because the weather is harsh or food scarce in the world in which they live. If animals did not die, there would soon be too little space and food to support them.

Animals grow, reproduce, and die. New animals are born. The new animal carries into the future the characteristics of the parent animal and passes them on to the next generation.

Plants make their own food, using the energy supplied by the sun and the chemicals supplied by the soil. Animals grow and develop by eating plants and other animals. The remains of the bodies of dead animals break down in the earth just as plants do. And, in so doing, they too may supply food for new plants and animals.

The chain of life continues. Each new living thing becomes a link in the chain, carrying part of the past into the future.

HUMAN BEINGS

The human life cycle follows the same pattern as that of plants and other animals: birth, growth and maturity, reproduction, aging, and death.

Human beings begin life as a fertilized egg in the mother's womb, an organ inside her body. The *embryo*, or *fetus*, as the developing individual is called, forms within the womb until birth takes place, after about nine months.

A period of growth follows that lasts approximately twenty years and takes us through infancy and childhood, the years of play and school; and *puberty*, or *adolescence*, our teen-age years. Our sexual life begins. In America, girls begin to menstruate at an average age of 12½ and are capable of reproducing. Boys can become fathers at 13.

At about 20, our bodies reach full maturity and we achieve our maximum size and strength. The next ten years are, physically, the peak of our lives. Our growth has mostly ended and our bodies have not yet begun to show signs of age.

AGING

Aging begins at birth. We start to grow old from the moment we are born, but changes start at different times in different parts of the body and proceed at different rates. Until the age of 30, our rate of growth offsets our rate of aging. Afterwards, the body wears down faster than it is able to grow and repair itself.

After 30, signs of aging usually begin to appear. Our skin doesn't fall back into place as well as it once did. It may begin to sag. Lines and wrinkles may appear on our faces. The lens of the eye may not bend and focus properly and we will need glasses. Our blood may not flow, or circulate, through the body as well as before. This affects our brain, nerves, senses, and digestion. Between 40 and 60, our hair may become thin or turn gray. In later years, we may have problems with our teeth and even need new ones.

Menopause, when menstruation ends, occurs at about age 50 in women. (Men, at about the same age, may experience complaints similar to those which some women have.) With menopause, women lose their ability to reproduce; sexuality, however, continues as a life-long capacity of women and men alike.

As we age, our muscles may not be as flexible as they once

were, making it harder for us to stretch and touch our toes. We are not as strong. It takes more effort to lift a heavy weight. Our endurance decreases. We can't jog as many miles or play as many sets of tennis.

The shapes of our bodies change as we age. In later years, we may stoop and bend and actually become shorter, as our spines lose their flexibility. When our bones become brittle, we may break our hips, arms, or legs if we fall.

We are less able to fight off sickness and disease as we grow old. This may be because our *immune system* breaks down. Illnesses which did not bother us as young people may trouble us when we are old.

Sometime after the age of 60, we become "officially" old. People over 62 can collect Social Security, or "old age insurance." Some towns issue "Senior Citizen" cards, which are passes to recreation areas such as beaches and golf courses; some stores give elderly people special discounts on certain days.

Yet, even though we are "officially" old, we need not cease to be productive. Many people choose to retire around 65, but increasing numbers prefer to stay on the job. By law, no one can make us retire until the age of 70, and not at all in certain occupations. Recent studies show that older workers are often more efficient, reliable, and creative than younger ones; that their vocabulary and ability to accumulate knowledge actually improves; and that people are happier if they *never* retire.

It is true, however, that as we age, we slow down. Our bodies slow down. We move more slowly. We think more slowly. This need not occur until our seventies or eighties, though; and, even when it does occur, it does not mean that we are any less intelligent or mentally sound.

Clockwise: Albert Einstein at 72; Georgia O'Keefe at 82;
George Burns at 80; Arthur Fiedler at 84; Pablo Picasso at 75.

"LATE MIDDLE AGE"

Everyday we read of people in their seventies, eighties, and even nineties who are still going strong. George Burns celebrated his eightieth birthday with an hour-long TV special, and never missed a cue! Arthur Fiedler conducted his fiftieth-anniversary concert with the Boston Pops Orchestra in his eighty-fourth year; Georgia O'Keefe was still painting at 91; and pianist and composer Eubie Blake celebrated his ninety-sixth birthday at a performance of the Broadway show *Eubie,* based on his life. Such people are not really "old" at all. Let's say they're enjoying a "late middle age."

HONORING
THE ELDERLY

In primitive cultures, the aged are honored because, being closer to death, they are also closer to their ancestors and to the spirit world, the forces which are believed to govern the life and well-being of the living. They are looked up to as a source of power and influence and much admired for their wisdom and experience, understanding, and judgment.

In the past, old people usually lived with the young until their death, contributing to the life of the family, and providing knowledge, comfort, and guidance to its younger members.

Today, in our country particularly, we tend to turn old people out, and confine them to nursing or retirement homes. This leads to a lack of understanding of the problems of old age and develops a tendency to think of old people as "sick" and even *"senile"* (without their mental faculties).

It is important that we understand that this is not necessarily true.

DEATH

At some point, death will come, as it does to all living things, to end the human life span. It may happen at any age. Many deaths occur at birth. Some, in infancy. The ages between 5 and 15 are the safest years in a person's life, probably because we are best protected and cared for then. Accidents in cars take the lives of many young people between 15 and 24. And over 700,000 young Americans have died in wars, in this century alone. But more and more of us are living to old age.

After the age of 40, the number of deaths doubles every eight years. (Still, if you reach the age of 65, you have a very good chance of living another sixteen years, to 81.) The chances of a person's dying at 85 are one hundred times greater than at 35.

When too many animals or plants live, they die from lack of food or space or from disease or even from poisons that their own bodies produce under overpopulated conditions.

In our world today, if human beings did not die, there would soon not be enough food, water, or space for everyone. And, there would not be enough energy in the world to supply all our needs. (Exciting possibilities may lie ahead, however. Colonies in space could expand our living areas.)

Human beings, like all other living things, round out their lives with death, forming a link in the chain of life with the generations that have gone before and those that will follow.

The individual dies, but life goes on as new individuals are born.

LONGEVITY

Some members of the plant and animal kingdoms live longer than others. *Longevity* means long life. The record for longevity in the plant world is held by the bristlecone pines of the White Mountains of California which live to be nearly 5,000 years old. They are the oldest living things known.

Among the *invertebrates,* animals without backbones, the ocean quahog, a type of mollusk, lives for 150 years. Among the *vertebrates,* the division of the animal kingdom to which human beings belong, reptiles (including snakes and lizards, turtles, and crocodiles) have the longest lives. Some tortoises live as long as 175 years! Human beings are the longest living mammals.

Scientists are not sure why some animals live longer than others. Often the larger animals live longer but that is not always true. People and parrots live longer than horses. Some turtles live longer than human beings.

It may be that the life span of an animal increases with size because smaller animals give off more internal heat in relation to their body's volume. This causes their hearts to work harder. (A small animal like a mouse, for instance, may have the same number of heartbeats in its lifetime as an elephant that lives thirty times as long!)

Another theory of longevity is that the bigger the brain of the animal in relation to its body, the longer the animal lives. The brain takes up a bigger proportion of a human being's body than that of a horse, an elephant, or a whale. A larger brain gives an animal better control over its body. It gets better messages from its eyes and nose and other senses and sends better messages to its muscles. In these ways, it is better able to cope

14

with dangers that threaten and changes that occur in the world around it.

The ocean quahog and the sea tortoise may live long lives because their environments change very little over the course of their lifetimes. Few adjustments are necessary.

Human Longevity

Some people, like some plants and other species of animals, live longer than others.

A tendency to longevity is inherited. That means, if your grandparents live to be one hundred years old, you have a good chance of doing it, too.

In some mountainous regions of Ecuador, Tibet, and the USSR, people claim to reach ages of 130 and 140 years and consider 100 the normal life span. This may be heredity. Or, it may be because they work outdoors in the mountains. The climate is cool and they get a lot of exercise. Their diet is low in calories and animal fats. They like their work and work as long as they want to. Old people, in these societies, are very much admired by the young.

Some bodies stay in good working order longer than others. Some bodies resist illness and disease better than others. Although these qualities may be inherited, we can live our lives in ways that help us live longer, too.

Every year, 350,000 people die in the United States from causes related to cigarette smoking. Nearly 50,000 people die in automobile accidents. An estimated 100,000 die of causes related to alcoholism.

We shouldn't stuff ourselves with food, or drink too much.

We need properly nourishing foods, avoiding too much sugar, animal fat, and salt. Regular exercise helps burn off extra fat and also prevents it from developing.

Some of the threats to our lives come from pollution of the air and water and earth around us. Carbon monoxide from automobiles and other combustion engines is poisonous. Excessive noise, which often occurs in our cities, can harm us physically and psychologically. Our highly industrialized society produces vast amounts of waste which threaten many forms of life. But pollution need not be inevitable. We are now becoming aware of the seriousness of the problem, and are taking measures to deal with it at the urging of concerned individuals, public officials, environmental groups, scientists, and technicians.

As we grow older, emotional upsets and tension may strain our hearts. We must be willing to adjust to change. We are more apt to live into the future if we have an *interest* in the future and an interest in others, as well.

Another theory of longevity is that the more satisfied you are with your life in your early years, the longer you will live in your later years.

The kind of work you do is important. Liking your work is important, too. The sculptor Michelangelo lived to be 89 at a time when the average lifetime was 35 years. Benjamin Franklin was 83 when he invented bifocal eyeglasses. Pablo Picasso died at 92. Symphony orchestra conductor Arturo Toscanini died at 90. Winston Churchill, at 91. American industrialist John D. Rockefeller lived to be 98.

Finally, the quality of the life we live is important.

Mrs. Eleanor Robson Belmont, who celebrated her one hundredth birthday in 1979, said, "It's doing what you want and doing it happily." She also gave an added tip, "I belong to that group of people who move the piano themselves."

In other words, people who live happy, full, and active lives are likely to live longer, too.

LIFE EXPECTANCY

How long do people live? Ancient historians, writing over two thousand years ago in the Bible, gave a human being's full *life expectancy*—the average number of years a person can expect to live—as "threescore years and ten," or seventy. It has taken hundreds of thousands of years for human life to reach that span but people can count on it now in only a few countries.

In prehistoric times, the average lifetime was 18 years, and death usually came from violent causes. In Caesar's Rome, the average was 22 years. The expected lifetime in the American colonies was 35. You could not expect to live beyond 40 until the nineteenth century. In 1900, the average lifetime in the United States was only 47. But, by 1950, it had climbed to 68 years.

We have gained a greater life expectancy in our century than in all past centuries combined!

Today, in the United States, the average life expectancy is 73 years. You can expect to live longer (77 years) if you are a woman. Men live, on average, 69 years.

People live longer in Western Europe and North America than in Latin America, Asia, or Africa. And people tend to live longer if they are rich rather than poor, married rather than single, live in a cool climate rather than hot, and in the country rather than the city.

17

WHY PEOPLE LIVE
LONGER TODAY

People live longer today because they live better today. And people who live in the richer and more industrial countries—like the United States and the countries of Western Europe—live longer than those who don't.

We have better houses than the Greeks and Romans did. We are better protected from the weather. We have warm clothes. We can turn on the oil or gas burner when it's cold. We no longer fear wild animals or dangerous enemies as prehistoric people did. Fire and police departments help to protect us and our homes.

In other times, plagues, famines, and natural disasters killed whole populations. *Infant mortality,* or the death of children under one year, was a major cause of death. Better education on how to care for infants and access to better medical care have changed this, particularly in the advantaged nations. But poor countries still have high rates of infant mortality: 15.1 per 1,000 births in the United States, 122.0 per 1,000 in India.

In the United States, we have better food and more of it than people did in medieval France or than many people in India, Asia, and parts of South America do today. Our food contains the necessary vitamins. Our drinking water is usually pure (and there is plenty of it). So is our milk.

Improved sanitation methods help to prevent disease. The garbage collector comes regularly. Our hospitals are clean and well equipped and use special chemicals as *disinfectants* to keep away germs.

Developed countries like the United States and Denmark and Sweden and Great Britain and Germany have good public health systems. Shots, or *inoculations,* prevent disease and stop it from spreading. So does insect control. Typhoid fever, diphtheria, and polio used to be killers. They are no longer. *Vaccinations* have wiped out smallpox. Few people worry about yellow fever anymore. There are shots for measles and German measles and a test for tuberculosis.

People long ago used wild plants and herbs to cure disease. Today, drugs called *antibiotics* help to prevent as well as cure it. The development of *penicillin* saved many lives in World War II.

A good public health system can make it possible for everyone to take advantage of new methods of disease control. A good education system can teach us good habits of eating and health care. Some countries provide free medical and dental care for all their citizens. But poor nations often lack the necessary funds. And, even in wealthy countries like the United States, not everyone can afford the medicine and food and vitamins they need to stay healthy and live longer.

Most ancient people thought that sickness, like death, was caused by evil spirits or angry gods. The science of medicine has come a long way since the fifth century B.C. when a Greek doctor named Hippocrates said that he believed illness came from natural causes.

Anesthetics that kill pain make it possible for doctors to perform long and difficult operations. New methods of surgery help to repair broken bones and even to replace or reattach fingers, hands, arms, and legs. Since 1954, ten thousand kidneys and eye corneas have been *transplanted* (transferred from one body to another); and, since 1967, about two hundred hearts. Lungs, livers, skin, and bone marrow have been taken from one body and put into another, extending lives.

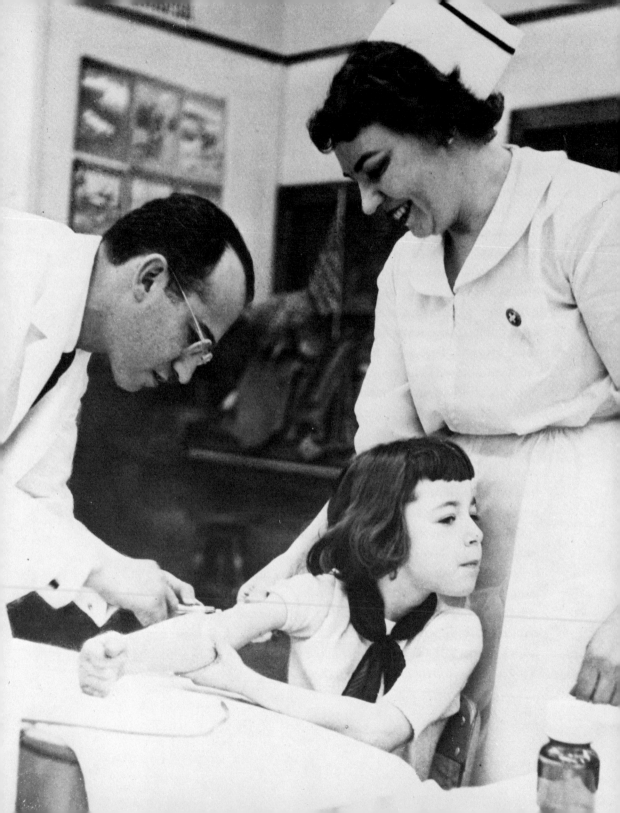

A new medical aid called a *stress test* measures how well our heart performs under physical exertion.

A machine can drain our blood, clean, and recycle it. Another machine can do the work of the heart while doctors perform open-heart surgery.

Some people have such faith in the advances of medicine that they are asking their doctors to freeze their bodies at death and to preserve them until some future time when a cure has been found for the illness or disease that caused them to die. Like a bear that hibernates in the winter, they hope to be brought back to life at a later time and live on. Their motto is, "Never say die!" This process is called *cryonics*. The frozen body is said to be in *cryonic suspension*. Some people have been willing to pay as much as $20,000 to maintain a body in this state even though scientists consider the cryonics theory "extremely doubtful" and, of course, no one has been brought back to life yet by using this process.

OUR AGING POPULATION

In former times many children died at birth and in infancy. Mothers, too, died in childbirth. Now, diseases that once caused death at an early age have been eliminated or brought under control and there are many more old people in our population.

Dr. Jonas Salk administers vaccine that he developed in 1953 to prevent poliomyelitis (infantile paralysis).

21

Improved sanitation helps us prevent death-causing diseases; inoculation and immunization help us control them; advances in medical science help us treat them; good school and public health systems keep us informed about them.

The major causes of death are no longer the *communicable,* or *infectious,* diseases (like influenza, typhoid, tuberculosis) that once killed most people before they reached old age. Childhood diseases (like whooping cough and scarlet fever) are under control. Newborn babies have better care.

The principal causes of death today are those which usually strike older people: diseases of the heart, cancer, and stroke. (One major exception is accidents. Americans still kill themselves in cars at the rate of nearly 50,000 per year.)

At the beginning of our century, one-half of the population used to die by the age of 40. Now, one-half of the people live past 70!

Eleven percent of the population of the United States—or 24 million people—is over 65. This will probably increase to 15 percent by the year 2000. There are 11,000 Americans over 100 years old today.

The ancient Egyptians considered 110 years the ideal life span. Although few of them lived to reach that age, it is possible that many of us will. It is also possible that future generations will not show the signs of aging that our parents and grandparents do.

We are not sure *why* the process of aging occurs, but it happens to all living things at more-or-less the same degree. Some scientists think there is a time clock built into our bodies that accounts for it. They are studying ways to reset the time clock so aging will not occur.

Gerontology, the science that deals with aging, suggests that the most typical signs of aging—the decline of vitality and physical fitness—may not have to occur at all. Research in this field is so promising that, in future generations, people may well lead vigorous, happy, healthy, and productive lives—free of illness and infirmity—until the day they die.

Old age may be a disease that can be cured; and, in the world of the future, you may not have to "grow old" when you grow old.

Science is learning many new ways to control disease and to deal with the symptoms of aging. Possibilities are being explored by researchers in biochemistry, bionics, genetics, temperature control, and transplantation.

Biochemistry. "Anti-aging" pills or injections may be developed. New drugs could improve a failing immune system; cellular research could lead to the production of cells that fight disease and prevent the breakdown of other cells. Improvements in diet habits, mental health, and the quality of the environment can also prevent aging. So can medical science. When cancer, heart, and lung diseases are brought under control, accidents may be the only remaining cause of death.

Bionics. Bionic technology may be expanded so that, in addition to the artificial eyes, intestines, arms, hips, and ankles available today, we will be able to replace the blood supply. Or, machines may be developed that will take the place of worn-out organs, including the heart, kidney, and pancreas. And newer will probably be better.

Genetics. Scientists are studying our *genes,* the parts of cells that determine how we develop and grow. Someday they may be able to change our genes so we can avoid disease entirely.

Temperature control. Lower body temperature slows our metabolism which may, in turn, slow the aging process. *Biofeedback* training, with the aid of electrical devices, can help us control this. Or, humans might learn to hibernate as many animals do.

Transplants. This field is expanding rapidly. Organs, bones, and tissues may be frozen for transplant, in the future. One scientist has proposed that we preserve bodies, called "neomorts," whose life is maintained by machine, to make up "organ farms" to supply healthy replacements for the living.

Many gerontologists believe that the mental and physical vigor of youth can be retained throughout our lifetime and that the normal life span can be extended to 150 years. Others predict we will live to be 300, 500, or even 800 years old! The biblical age of Methuselah was 969.

LIFE AND DEATH

It is as natural to man to die,
as it is to be born.

Francis Bacon

Life has existed on earth in some form for 3.7 billion years. Human beings are a fairly recent development in this endless chain. But, our ancestors were probably alive as long as 2.5 million years ago.

What does it mean to be alive? And, how is it different from *not* being alive?

LIFE

First of all, living things move. Fish swim in a lake. Birds fly. Kids play stickball in the street. Even plants move, although they do it so slowly it's barely noticeable.

Living things respond to their *environment,* the world around them. A plant responds to the sunshine by growing toward the light. A dog responds to midsummer heat by lying in the shade. We put on a coat or turn up the heat when we feel winter's cold. An animal runs from danger. If necessary, living things can change to meet changing conditions in their environment: the fins of some fish developed into legs when they lived on land; the legs of whales became flippers when they moved into the water.

Living things grow. We grow by taking in food in the form of plant or other animal life. Egg salad sandwiches help us to grow. So does the fruit of a cherry tree. And the meat from a steer which has been grazing on plant life in the field. Our bodies break down food to produce the energy we need for growth and movement.

All living things, including human beings, have the ability to reproduce, to make more of their own kind. That is how they make sure that the *species,* or group, to which they belong will continue for future generations. It is also the way they pass on the changes they make in adapting to the world around them.

The Basic Unit of Life
The basic unit of all living things is the *cell,* a mass so small that a drop of blood the size of a pinhead contains over 5 million of them!

Some kinds of cells group together to form *tissues,* like the skin that covers our body; the muscles that move our parts; the cartilage, bone, and fat that support our body; and the nerve tissue that carries messages to and from our brain.

Groups of tissues clustered together form the *organs,* including our heart, brain, stomach, liver, lungs, and sense organs like our eyes, ears, mouth, and nose. They work to keep the body running.

Some simple plants and animals (like the *amoeba* and

paramecium) are one-celled organisms. A single cell performs all their bodily functions.

The human body, however, has something like 60 trillion cells! And each cell has its own job. Some cells help us see; some help us digest our food; some carry instructions from our brain to our muscles; and so on.

We grow and develop as these cells grow. Some of them grow by increasing in number; some of them increase in size. As the parts grow, so does our whole body. As we grow, cells wear out and are replaced by new cells. Some cells die and are not replaced. Some of the new cells may not work as well as the old ones.

The cells also take in food, break it down, and digest it. Growth comes from this process, called *metabolism*. Energy also comes from this process, the energy we need to be able to move and respond with our senses to our environment.

The cells supply the materials for repairing and rebuilding our tissues. The food that the cells absorb nourishes our tissues and organs, our skin and muscles, our livers and lungs.

Plants make their own food, from water and chemicals in the earth and air, by using the energy of the sun. Animals can't make their own food although they can convert stored food, in the form of fat, into energy. They must feed on plants or other animals that eat plants to get the substances they need to supply their energy and ensure growth.

DEATH

How does a dead being differ from a live one? Perhaps you have seen a dead animal. A pet canary or gerbil may have died. Or, you may have seen a dead dog or cat that has been hit by a car and is lying on the road. It is very different from a live animal.

A dead animal doesn't move. It doesn't come when you call or wag its tail or purr when you stroke it. If you try to lift it, it goes limp. It droops and sags and doesn't hold its proper shape. A dead animal cannot control or move its muscles. Its head flops from side to side instead of standing upright on its spine. Or, if it has been dead for several hours, its muscles may have tightened and its body become stiff. This is called *rigor mortis* ("the stiffness of death") which lasts about twenty-four hours. If the animal has been dead for a longer period, it will begin to smell as its body starts to break down and decay. Its body will decompose just as the dead plant decomposed before it became part of the earth again.

A person who is dead doesn't move, either. Dead people don't respond to the world around them as they did in life. They don't hear sounds or feel a pinch or a pinprick. Their knees don't jerk when the doctor taps them. A bright light held in front of the eye will not cause the pupil to contract. Changes in temperature don't affect them. Their own body temperature drops to that of the air around them and their bodies are cold. Because blood no longer flows freely through their body, it may settle under the skin in purple blotches. The mouth, lips, toes, and fingertips may turn blue.

Except for hair and fingernails, which continue to grow for several hours after death, growth has ended. Metabolism has stopped.

What has caused the change? What has happened to change a living body into a dead one?

Biological Death

We know that the body is made up of billions of cells. These cells get their food from the blood that the heart pumps to them through the veins and arteries. The blood also carries oxygen to the cells.

Something may cut off this blood supply: a heart attack may stop the heart from pumping blood; a growth, or cancer, may block its passage through the circulatory system; a stroke may cause a clot or block to form; a severe accident—like that which happened to the dog on the highway—may damage the blood vessels or cause a swelling which blocks them.

Death, like the processes of birth and growth and aging, happens in stages.

When the heart stops, death has begun. This is called *clinical death*.

Without the flow of blood from the heart, the cells of the body no longer receive the supply of food and oxygen they need and they begin to die. The *cerebral* cells in the front part of the brain die first. They are the cells that control our ability to learn and remember, to reason, to understand and communicate. They are the cells that control all our conscious actions.

Some cells of the body begin to die as soon as we are born. The cells in our brain and muscles decrease in number as we age. Some of the body's cells, those of the skin and hair, for instance, can repair or replace themselves. Some cannot. The cells of the brain cannot repair or replace themselves.

Damage to the cerebral cells, or *brain damage,* takes place within four to six minutes after the heart stops, cutting off their supply of oxygen. If the heart can be started again, during this short time, the cells may be saved. But, after about ten minutes without oxygen, they can almost never be effectively restored.

The heart may beat again and breathing may take place. The body may digest food and perform actions that do not require conscious, or *voluntary*, effort on the part of the brain. But, the body will not feel sensations or react or respond. It will be in a state of *coma*, or unconsciousness.

Death of the brain cells that control the *involuntary* actions of the body comes next.

Complete *brain death* takes place with the absence of oxygen to the brain for about fifteen minutes.

A heart may be made to beat again, but brain death cannot be reversed.

Death of the other cells of the body follows brain death: those of the other organs and tissues, the glands, muscles, and skin. Finally, after about forty-eight hours, the body begins to decompose.

Defining Death

The Pygmies of the African Congo recognize five stages of illness and death: hot, ill, dead, completely dead, and dead forever. How can we tell when a person is really dead?

The legal definition of death, which was set in 1890, is simply the ending of life, identified by a doctor as the total stopping of the circulation of blood and the absence of breathing, heartbeat, and pulsation for a certain period of time, usually thirty minutes to an hour.

In the past, doctors used simple tests to determine death by this simple definition. They might place a mirror or a feather at the lips or nose of the dying person. If the glass clouded over or the feather moved, the person was still breathing and, therefore, alive.

The doctor's ear, or an instrument called a *stethoscope,* was placed over the heart to hear the heartbeat; a finger, placed on the pulse, to feel it.

Today, we have more complicated instruments. A machine called an *electrocardiograph* (EKG) measures the heartbeat; an *electroencephalograph* (EEG) records the waves sent out by the brain and tells us whether the brain cells are still alive.

Defining death has become more complicated, too. Electric shock, chemical stimulation, mouth-to-mouth resuscitation, artificial respiration, and heart massage can restore breathing. A *respirator* can maintain breathing and keep the blood flowing even after the brain has died. New blood can be pumped into the veins by *transfusion.* Oxygen can be supplied. Medicine can keep infection away. Feeding can take place through the veins, or *intravenously.*

The heart and lungs can be made to work even though the brain does not.

This is important today when we have learned how to replace kidneys, eyes, and hearts by transplanting them from one body to another. These organs can be kept alive for about half an hour after brain death. This gives doctors time to pass them on to living persons while they are still usable.

But, first, the doctor must be able to say that the donor of the organ is dead, and to define the moment when death occurs.

Eleven states are now defining death as brain death. Under the law passed by Maryland in 1972, a person is considered dead if heartbeat and breathing no longer take place naturally, attempts at reviving them are considered hopeless, and there is no brain activity.

If the heart and lungs can't work on their own without the help of a respirator, and no brain waves appear on the EEG, death is certain.

When death is defined as brain death, doctors can—with consent—remove the organs of the body while they are still functioning and transplant them into another living body.

Life Support

Measures that keep a person alive by artificial means are called *life support* or *life-sustaining* efforts. And, sometimes, "medicated survival."

Life support raises many questions which have not yet been answered. Who should have the machines when there are not enough to go around? The young, the old, or only those who can afford to pay the high cost of running them? Who should have the few organs available for transplant? Who should decide when to stop life support efforts? Are these efforts really maintaining life or do they interfere with the natural process of dying, perhaps prolonging suffering?

California passed a law in 1976 which states that doctors can be ordered to disconnect life-sustaining equipment if it only serves to artificially prolong the moment of death. This may be the law of the future.

There is another important question. Who should decide when to end life support measures? Should it be a doctor or a lawyer or the family of the dying person? Or a combination of all three? If the person follows a special religion, perhaps the minister or priest or rabbi should be asked, too.

It isn't easy for doctors alone to make the decision to end life support because they have sworn to follow the Hippocratic Oath to do everything possible to cure the sick and sustain life.

Some people think the dying person should decide. In fact, eight states recognize the right to decide in advance. The California law, called the Natural Death Act, allows a person to write a "living will," asking that unusual or artificial measures not be used to continue life when death is inevitable. The family of a dying person may also request this.

Laws that permit people to refuse medical treatment when they are dying are called laws for the "right to die" or "death with dignity."

Euthanasia

It is not far from letting a person die—called *orthothanasia*—to helping a person die—called *euthanasia,* from the Greek words for "good" and "death."

Euthanasia got a bad name from its use in ancient Sparta when deformed or retarded children were thrown from mountaintops; and, in our time, from Nazi Germany where mass executions were sometimes called mercy killings.

In 1938, Charles Francis Potter, a minister, founded the Euthanasia Society of America. It is now called the Society for the Right to Die.

Active euthanasia is against the law in all states in this country, but some other countries—Germany, Norway, Switzerland, and Uruguay—do not consider it a crime.

A LIVING WILL

To my family, my physician, my lawyer, my clergyman
To any medical facility in whose care I happen to be
To any individual who may become responsible for my health, welfare or
affairs

*Death is as much a reality as birth, growth, maturity and old age — it is
the one certainty of life. If the time comes when I
                        can no longer take part in decisions for my own
future, let this statement stand as an expression of my wishes, while I
am still of sound mind.*

*If the situation should arise in which there is no reasonable expectation
of my recovery from physical or mental disability, I request that I be
allowed to die and not be kept alive by artificial means or "heroic measures." I do not fear death itself as much as the indignities of deteriora-
tion, dependence and hopeless pain. I, therefore, ask that medication be
mercifully administered to me to alleviate suffering even though this may
hasten the moment of death.*

*This request is made after careful consideration. I hope you who care
for me will feel morally bound to follow its mandate. I recognize that this
appears to place a heavy responsibility upon you, but it is with the intention of relieving you of such responsibility and of placing it upon my-
self in accordance with my strong convictions, that this statement is made.*

*Signed*_____

Date_____

Witnessed by:

_____   _____

*"A Living Will" requests that "heroic measures"
not be used to prevent death when there is no
reasonable chance for recovery.*

If a person is near death and cannot be brought back to a meaningful life, if the pain of the illness is unbearable, or if the brain is so damaged that a person is totally paralyzed, or, so badly deformed that a normal life is impossible, should he or she be helped to die? Should people who have a *terminal,* or final, illness from which there is no hope of recovery, be allowed to die when they wish?

Many people oppose active euthanasia because they think it is against the will of God or because they believe that no human being has the right to take away the life of another. There are questions of law and medicine and theology to be considered.

Passive euthanasia may be widely practiced, but to favor active euthanasia is still an extreme position.

Suicide, or taking one's own life, is also illegal in most places. It is another form of death in which individuals make their own choices. Should people be permitted to make this decision when a meaningful life is no longer possible for them? When mental or physical illness, or unhappiness, become unbearable, should we let people die if they want to? Most people oppose making suicide legal because, with proper treatment, most suicides can be averted. Help is available and should be sought.

When Alexander the Great asked how long one should live, an adviser replied: "As long as one does not prefer death to life."

But, for us today, as for many generations in the past, there are no easy answers.

BURIAL CUSTOMS
OF THE PAST

Human beings have held special ceremonies for their dead since prehistoric times. Sometimes, because they feared the dead. Sometimes, because they wished to honor them. Sometimes, because they wished to prepare them for a future life in another world; or, to win favor with the gods.

Human beings are the only animal species that buries its dead. Death, like birth and marriage, is a very important event in human lives, calling for a very important ceremony.

In the Old Stone Age, possibly as long as 50,000 years ago, Neanderthal people buried their dead with tools, weapons, ornaments, and sometimes food. They arranged animal skulls in the form of an altar or sheltered their graves in rocks or caves or fenced them in with the horns of goats or the bones of huge mammoths.

A Neanderthal grave found in Iraq in 1968 held a body lying on a bed of pine branches with the remains of flowers placed about it. We are not sure whether this was a sign of love and respect or an attempt to sweeten the smell of the decomposing body.

Cro-Magnon people decorated the bodies of the dead with a red dye, perhaps in imitation of blood in hopes of bringing the dead back to life.

Primitive people usually feared the dead and sometimes thought that death might be "catching." They thought that the spirit of the dead could come back to the world of the living, probably to do harm. This belief determined many of the early burial customs. The first tombstones, placed over the grave, may have been put there to keep the spirit of the dead from roaming.

Bodies were often buried with their knees bent and arms pressed to their chests. This may have been meant to resemble the birth position, from which the dead might be reborn; or to look like a body in sleep, which primitive people confused with death, and from which they thought the dead might awaken. Or, it may have been an attempt to restrain the bodies from rising from death and returning to harm the living.

Peking people, 40,000 years ago, *ate* their dead in what may have been a sign of respect, to preserve the good qualities of the dead in the living.

In addition to *interment,* or burial in the ground, another method of disposal practiced by primitive people was *exposure.* Rather than bury the dead body, they left it on a rock or high in a tree where it was exposed to wild animals, birds of prey, and the weather.

The ancient Egyptians, 6,000 years ago, developed elaborate means to preserve the body which, they believed, went on to life in another world after death.

The insides of the dead body were removed and it was preserved, or *embalmed,* in wrappings of linen bandages, sometimes twenty layers thick, covered with layers of wax or resin. The process took seventy days.

The mummy was placed in a coffin, or series of coffins, decorated with beautifully colored paintings. There was an outer stone coffin called a *sarcophagus*.

Preservation was important to the Egyptians because, like all ancient people, they believed that the body lived on after death. Mummification prepared the dead for its afterlife in the tomb or for the journey to another world. Egyptian kings, or *pharaohs,* were buried in hidden tombs in the Valley of the Kings along the Nile River, or in impressive stone pyramids. All the needs of life, sometimes including the slaves to serve him, were buried with the pharaoh in his tomb.

(There are modern pharaohs, too. A Texas oil heiress was buried in San Antonio in 1977, dressed in her lace nightgown and seated in the driver's seat of her 1964 Ferrari! The grave was then filled with concrete to prevent vandalism.)

The Vikings, ancestors of today's Scandinavians, were sea-faring people who buried their kings in boats with high prows, then set them out to sea for the voyage to the other world. We sometimes bury people at sea today, especially sailors who have died aboard ship in wartime.

The ancient Scythians, who lived 2,500 years ago in what is now part of Russia, built huge underground tombs of many rooms where they buried their warriors, embalmed with roots and herbs. They also buried their horses and the grooms to care for them. And, sometimes, even their wives went along.

Burial customs tell us a great deal about how people lived in other times. A 12,000-year-old grave found in Israel revealed a man buried with his hand on a young puppy, showing that dogs were kept as pets that long ago!

THE MODERN FUNERAL

Today, when someone dies, there are laws in most countries that tell us what to do.

In the United States, if a person dies at home, a doctor must be called at once. The doctor declares the person dead and enters the medical history, including time, place, and cause of death, on a *death certificate*. When death happens in a hospital, or nursing home, the certificate is completed there.

Death certificates help us to compile *Vital Statistics,* the official record of births, marriage and divorce, death and its causes. The practice began centuries ago in China. In England and America, in times past, churches kept these records.

If a dead person has not been under a doctor's care, or if death is sudden or accidental, suicide or murder, the town medical examiner, or *coroner,* is called to confirm death. An investigation called an *inquest* may be held when the causes of death are unknown, unclear, or suspicious.

AUTOPSY

Sometimes, an *autopsy,* or *postmortem* (meaning "after death") examination is requested. The word *autopsy* comes from the ancient Greek words meaning, "to see with one's own eyes," and the Greeks were the first to perform autopsies, in the third century B.C. Autopsies made possible many of the advances of modern medicine.

In an autopsy, the body is cut open and studied. The organs are removed, dissected, and examined under a microscope, and the body tissues and fluids chemically tested.

Postmortem examinations help train doctors. They sometimes show that mistakes in *diagnosis,* or analysis of the cause of death, have been made. In fact, 30 percent to 50 percent of the stated reasons for death are found to be incorrect after an autopsy!

Autopsies help an inquest because they reveal bullet wounds, needle marks, cuts, and bruises which might not otherwise be seen.

Autopsies also provide research which helps to prevent disease and to cure it; and to test the usefulness of drugs and medicines. And, when death comes from accidents in cars and airplanes, an autopsy sometimes helps to suggest future safety measures.

The percentage of autopsies has declined from 50 percent of all deaths in the United States in 1950 to only 20 percent today. Many doctors and scientists are urging that more of them be done. Except for murder and suicide and accidents involving the safety of others, autopsies often require the written permission of the dead person's family. In Sweden, autopsies are performed unless permission is specifically denied.

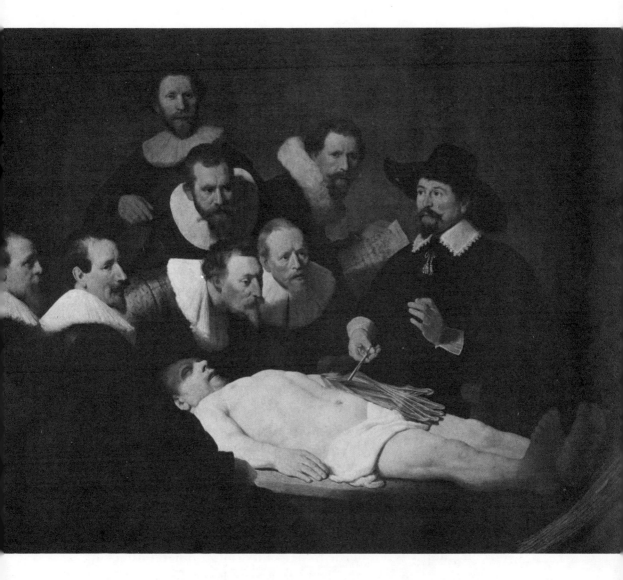

The Anatomy Lesson of Professor Tulp.
*Rembrandt painted this picture for the
Surgeons' Guild of Amsterdam in 1632.*

BODY DONATION

A living person can request that his or her body be donated after death for medical research and postmortem study. Written permission may also be given for the donation of organs—heart, eyes, kidneys—for transplant. In some states, you can indicate the intention to become an organ donor on your driver's license.

The first successful transplant of a human kidney was achieved at Peter Bent Brigham Hospital in Boston in 1954. Today, four thousand kidneys are transplanted every year in the United States and many more people are waiting for additional kidneys to become available. Dr. Christiaan Barnard performed the first heart transplant in South Africa in 1967. Today, about a hundred people are living with a heart that once belonged to someone else. Tens of thousands of corneas of the eye have been donated to make it possible for other people to see.

Fewer than 7,000 people a year of the nearly 2 million who die in the United States donate their bodies or parts of their bodies for these uses. Perhaps more will do so in the future. Most religions accept organ donation as a proper use of the body after death; although they do not always approve of an autopsy, because of their belief that the body is sacred.

THE FUNERAL HOME

When death occurs, if the cause of death has been determined and an autopsy is not needed, the family calls a funeral director, or *mortician,* to take the body from the home or hospital or nursing home to a funeral home. (Funeral directors haven't been called "undertakers" since 1885; calling them that today is like calling the doctor "sawbones" or a policeman "the fuzz.")

The funeral director completes the death certificate by providing additional information: place and date of birth, occupation, marital status, social security number, and so forth.

After the completed death certificate is filed with the proper town authorities, such as town clerk and board of health, permission for burial is granted.

Preparing the Body

In the United States, burials were once quite simple. The dead person was wrapped in a cloth called a *shroud,* put in a plain pine box, and buried in the ground. After the nineteenth century, they became more and more elaborate, leading to the charge that funeral homes often earn unnecessarily high fees by taking advantage of survivors at a difficult time. An oak coffin encased in bronze and fitted with sheets and pillows of satin can cost as much as $5,000. Consumer groups have worked to end abuses. Today, the funeral director must show the plain pine box as well.

Embalming

Embalming as a means of preserving dead bodies was a high art in ancient Egypt, 5,000 years ago. Mummies of embalmed Egyptian kings have survived in perfect condition for as long as 3,500 years! Ancient Greeks, Romans, and Hebrews rubbed dead bodies with spices, herbs, and oils; perhaps to soften the odor of decay as well as to preserve them. Today, in some places of South America where the climate is hot and dry, bodies left in rock shelters or caves are preserved naturally.

Embalming went out of favor with the Judeo-Christian religions because of their belief that the body is sacred and should not be touched after death.

Modern embalming began in the seventeenth century in Germany as a means of preserving the body and its parts for medical study. The process removes the blood and other fluids from the body and injects a solution of formaldehyde, mercury chloride, zinc chloride, and alcohol, which gives the skin a pinkish color similar to that of a living body.

Today, embalming is widely practiced only in Canada and the United States where it was revived in the nineteenth century to protect the bodies of soldiers killed in the Civil War while they were carried home from the battlefield for burial.

Modern embalming methods cannot prevent the eventual decomposition of the body; however, we do not know the secrets of the ancient Egyptians.

Embalming is required by law only under special conditions. Many states require embalming if burial does not take place within twenty-four or forty-eight hours or if death comes from a communicable disease. A body cannot usually be shipped across state lines by a commercial carrier without being embalmed. This means that someone dying in a state other than their own must be embalmed to travel home. (It is expensive to ship a dead body. It costs twice as much for a dead person to travel as it costs a living person.)

A body must also be embalmed for viewing in an open casket at a *visitation* in the funeral home or a *wake* in a Catholic home. The body of an important person is embalmed to lie "in state." In our time, popes and presidents, and even movie stars, have been seen in this way by thousands of people.

The body of V. I. Lenin, a founder of Russian Communism, who died in 1924, is a modern mummy. His specially preserved body lies in a tomb outside the Kremlin in Moscow. Each day, thousands of people file by to view it. Every few years the body is re-embalmed.

Embalming can restore bodies damaged by accident or disease. Cosmetic embalming—coloring the lips and cheeks—makes the dead person look more lifelike. Some people think this helps the survivors remember the dead person. Others feel it is more difficult for them to realize that death has occurred.

Some people believe embalming is necessary to prevent the spread of disease. However, few people die of infectious diseases today, and living bodies spread more disease than dead ones.

THE FUNERAL

We still dispose of our dead with ceremony, not because we fear them, but because we wish to honor them in a special way. Death, like birth and marriage, is an important social event in our society. The more important the person, the more impressive the ceremony.

The funeral is a *rite of passage,* a public ceremony at which we recognize death and dispose of the body of the dead. It also meets the needs of the living, helping them to face the reality of death, comforting them at a time of loss, and helping them adjust to a future life without the dead person.

Modern burial customs differ in different parts of the world and according to different religious practices.

In this country, some sort of visitation, where friends can

express feelings of sorrow and share memories of the dead, may precede the funeral ceremony.

The service may be held at the funeral home, in a church, or in the home of the family. The time and place must be set and, if the ceremony is to be a religious one, the clergyman consulted on choice of music, prayers, and sermon. Casket bearers, or *pallbearers,* and ushers are named.

The funeral home provides a car or *hearse* to carry the casket (be it plain pine or solid bronze) to the church and burial place, cars for the family, and a flower car. There is usually an escort car for the trip to the burial site, too. The average cost of a funeral in the United States today is about $2500.

Flowers are used less often now; they are considered by many to be expensive and wasteful. When his mother-in-law died in 1960, President Eisenhower asked that, instead of flowers, contributions be made to charity. People often feel this is a more permanent way to honor the dead and to continue their good works in life.

Sometimes the body is present for the funeral, sometimes not. A public memorial service may be held, before or after the body is buried in the presence of the family alone. Presence of the body helps some people accept the reality of death. Others feel uncomfortable with it there and find it depressing.

The Procession

After the service, the body is carried to the burial site. Throughout history, it has often been true that the more important the dead person has been in the life of the community, the more elaborate the funeral procession will be.

To honor their departed warrior-kings, the Scythians formed a funeral *cortege* or parade which went from village to village for forty days, acting out scenes from their lives. In ancient Rome, torchlight parades honored the important dead. The procession of an Egyptian pharaoh included a funerary boat, sometimes over 100 feet long, which carried the mummy to the tomb.

No one ever rides in a Muhammadan, or Muslim, procession because they believe that angels, accompanying the body, walk. Carrying the body is considered a good deed for Allah so everyone takes turns doing it.

The death of Winston Churchill was marked by an impressive ceremony in London. In our country, we have seen moving processions in honor of President John F. Kennedy, Senator Robert F. Kennedy, and the Reverend Martin Luther King, Jr.

Hawaiians follow their burials with a festive *luau.*

In New Orleans, funeral processions are accompanied by a jazz band which plays solemn music on the way to the burial and spirited marching songs like "When the Saints Come Marching In" on the way back. This both comforts the survivors in their grief and encourages them to accept death and get back to the world of the living with enthusiasm.

Whatever funeral customs are, they have developed because people felt they were helpful to the survivors in making the adjustments which the passage from life to death requires.

Some people avoid funerals because they find them upsetting, or because they do not approve of elaborate or expensive ceremonies. But people who believe in funerals feel they comfort the survivors by bringing together people, especially family and

*A solemn Grand Marshal leads the brass band
in a traditional New Orleans jazz funeral.*

friends, who may have been separated before death occurred. They also believe a funeral gives us a chance to show our love for each other as well as to pay public honor to the memory of the dead and that children, too, should be allowed to take part in the ceremonies, if they wish.

CREMATION

Increasing numbers of people are choosing to be cremated instead of buried in the ground. Cremation disposes of the dead body by fire.

Cremation has been practiced in some form since prehistoric times, when fire was used to purify the body or to destroy it so the dead could not return to harm the living. It was common in ancient Greece and Rome.

Wandering tribes, which left their dead behind, burned their bodies to prevent them from following in anger. The Vikings sometimes set fire to the funeral boats that they set out to sea. The Pygmies of the African Congo, and some American Indian tribes, bury their dead in the huts where they lived, then set fire to them.

Cremation is the accepted form of burial today among Buddhists and Hindus who believe it frees the soul to go on to another life after death.

In India, until it was forbidden in 1829, the wife of a dead man often threw herself on the funeral fire to be burned with her husband.

The first *crematorium* in the United States was built in 1876 by a doctor in Pennsylvania for the use of his family and friends. Today, cremation is used in about 8 percent of American deaths. Over half of the people who die in England are cremated, and most of the people in Japan, where land is very scarce. It is common in Denmark, Sweden, and Switzerland.

At the crematorium, the body and its casket are placed in an oven or furnace heated to 2,000 to 2,500 degrees Fahrenheit (1093 to 1371 degrees Celsius). The fire consumes the body in about an hour. The ashes that remain may be buried in the ground or spread about the home or other place of special importance to the dead person. Or, they may be placed in a container called an *ossuary* and preserved at home or in a space in a wall called a *columbarium,* at a special burial site.

Cremation is becoming more practiced in our time because there is little space in big cities for more cemeteries. Many people prefer it because they feel it is more sanitary and simpler than a ground burial. It is less expensive because there is no continuing upkeep and care of a burial site or need for an expensive headstone. (An organization in California, called the Neptune Society, picks up a body, cremates it, and scatters the ashes at sea for a fee of $270.)

When a body has been badly damaged by accident or disease, cremation disposes of it cleanly and quickly. It also avoids the slow decay of the body which occurs in the ground.

Some religious groups oppose cremation because they believe the body is sacred and cremation is *mutilation*. Some lawyers object to it because it may destroy evidence of crime.

Other people believe that committing the ashes to the earth is a fitting way to complete the cycle of individual life and to recycle the body for a new beginning in the continuing chain of nature.

LIFE AFTER DEATH

We still have no scientific studies to tell us what happens *after* death. But, most of the people of the world have always believed that some sort of life goes on. All the religions of the world were founded on this belief.

Many cultures believe that there is a soul which has a life separate from the body. The Egyptians called it the *ba*.

In most Western religions, people believe that death is not an ending but a beginning, that the soul lives on in another life after the death of the body. Life in our world is a preparation for the new life to come. Some believe that people are judged at death. Those who are good in life will be rewarded by going to a good place after death. Those who are bad will be punished by going to a bad place. Others do not accept the idea of punishment, but believe that a person's relationship with God continues after death and that the life of the spirit evolves in some form we may not understand. The dead person lives on, or survives, in the life of the soul.

In the religions of the East, living and dying are a spiral of continuing rebirth or *reincarnation*. The soul lives many lives in this world, sometimes in the same body, sometimes in a different one. One's present life is determined by its life on earth at a former time. After many lives, many deaths, and many rebirths, it achieves a final blessed state called *nirvana*, or *Brahma*. The dead person becomes one with the universe.

Jewish people believe that there may be an afterlife with punishment and rewards but that life in this world is more important. A person lives on after death by influencing other lives or the life of the community in which they lived. The dead person lives on in memory and in the lives of their children.

In spite of tremendous advances in knowledge in other areas, there are still many different theories about an afterlife. We may be confused ourselves. Or even fearful. Not everyone knows what to believe. Like the comedian Woody Allen, they might say, "I don't believe in an afterlife, although I am bringing a change of underwear."

Some people who have been close to death or whose hearts have stopped and been revived, report that the experience of death is a sensation like floating out of the body. After a period when they hear a loud buzzing noise like the roar in a tunnel, they are "lifted out of themselves."

They also report their life flashing before their eyes at the moment of death, a belief that was held in the Middle Ages. No one has reported feeling pain or fear. Some describe an encounter with a "being of light," in a warm loving place where friends and relatives are waiting.

Few scientists accept these experiences as proof of life after death. They say they are similar to the symptoms that occur in the state of elation, or *euphoria,* which results from a lack of oxygen. One psychiatrist thinks they may be recollections of the experience of being born.

People called *spiritualists* believe it is possible to communicate with people after they die. A special person called a *medium* helps to make contact.

GRIEF AND MOURNING

Truly it is allowed to weep . . .
By weeping we disperse our wrath

Ovid

When someone close to us dies, we feel sad. Sometimes we may feel angry, too. Angry and hurt that they have left us. We may also feel guilty and wonder if they died because of something we did or said. Did our dog die because we forgot to feed it? When we said in anger, "I wish you were dead!" did our wish come true and kill someone? Were *we,* in some way, responsible for their death?

We feel many different emotions, called *grief,* when someone dies, and we may forget, under stress, that death happens for a scientific reason. It is not caused by angry thoughts or spirits or magical bone-pointing or wishes or spells or curses. Even though we may feel guilty, our actions have nothing to do with it.

Old people die when their bodies wear down and the machinery that runs their bodies no longer works properly.

When a young person dies, there is a reason for it, too. A severe accident may have damaged the brain so badly that all conscious life has ended. A serious illness may have weakened and destroyed the body so that it can no longer function properly.

Death happens for a reason, although it is sometimes hard for us to understand the reason. We may understand "how," but we may not understand "why." And, even when we understand, we usually still feel grief. How much we feel depends on our feelings about the dead person.

Some animals other than humans show grief, too. Monkeys have been seen carrying the dead body of their young, hugging it, perhaps trying to bring it back to life. Elephants, too, show signs of sadness at death.

Grief is a sign of love. It shows we cared about the person who died.

We may have physical symptoms of grief: headache, dizziness, sleeplessness, loss of appetite, tightness of throat, and shortness of breath are some of them.

Crying helps us over our grief. It also helps to talk about our feelings and to know that others feel as we do. And, it helps to talk about the person who died.

A Swiss-born psychiatrist, Elisabeth Kübler-Ross, found that dying people go through five stages of grief and that we, as survivors, go through similar ones. At first, we may refuse to believe that death has come to someone we care about. We say, "No! This just can't be true!" We deny death. Then, we may be angry and ask, "*Why* has this happened to me?" Or, even, "Why have they *done* this to me?" We might try to bargain and say, "If they can only live a little longer" or "If they will only come back to me, I will be a better person." But, the bargaining fails, and we become sad and depressed. In the final stage of grief, we reach the stage of acceptance.

Grief, like death, is natural and necessary. Grief helps us work through all the confused feelings we have when someone dies. After a while, we will be able to accept their death and get on with living. Then, recalling the dead in memory can give us pleasure and help to guide our future.

When friends lose someone they care about, we should tell them we're sorry too. Sometimes we write a *letter of condolence* to express our sympathy.

Mourning

Over the centuries, mourning has taken many different forms. Special customs, costumes, and ceremonies have been part of the expressions of grief. The Maori of New Zealand wear wreathes of green leaves, cry loudly, and slash themselves with knives. Australian aborigines walk backward with their clothing inside out (because death is the opposite of life). In some South African tribes, women wander through the woods, wailing, waving their arms, and beating their breasts until they fall to the ground exhausted. The Pygmies of the Congo River Basin do a dance of death to try to make their forest happy again.

In China, mourners wear white instead of black. In Bali and Java, they smile or laugh instead of crying. Some people stop clocks, open or close windows, or cover mirrors.

In England, at the time of Queen Victoria, mourning dress included black bands on the hats and arms of men; black silk or lace dresses, trimmed with crepe and tulle, for the ladies; black braid, beads and buttons of jet. Mourning wreathes were hung on doorways, and horses with black plumes and feathers pulled elaborate hearses. Children, dressed in black and wearing black

top hats trailing "weepers," were hired to walk beside the hearse, carrying mourning parasols.

Some religions have definite rules for mourning. Among Buddhists and Hindus, ceremonies last for thirty-one to forty-nine days, while the soul of the dead travels between death and rebirth.

Catholics may observe strict mourning for three days while they *wake,* or watch, the dead. The Jewish *shiva* lasts for seven days and is followed by a period of partial mourning, *sh-loshim,* which lasts for a month, when survivors can work but can't go to places of public entertainment. Mourning for a parent or close relative lasts a full year.

Except for these customs, the length of the period of grief and mourning is not clearly defined in the United States today. Grief itself often lasts without relief for a full year. One full year of mourning takes one through all the changes of the seasons without the person who died. After that time, it may be easier to begin a new year adjusted to life without them.

Children under 13 are usually not required to take part in formal mourning. However, most people today believe that children should be allowed to take part in the mourning process if they wish; just as they should feel free to discuss the subject of death, and their feelings about it, with others.

A Congo mother crawls around her village on hands and knees crying and shrieking for her dying child.

A GOOD DEATH

In the Middle Ages, when a knight felt death approaching, he gathered his friends and family around him and prepared for its coming. Death was a ceremony in which the dying knight, lying in bed, recalled the events of his life and talked about the sadness of dying. If he had hurt anyone present, he asked their forgiveness. He then called for his priest, said his prayers and farewells, and silently and peacefully awaited his death.

This was a "good" or "fitting" death.

Today, a good death is one in which, as the functions of the body gradually slow down, we die in old age, feeling that our life and work have been satisfying and useful. We would like death to come without suffering, if possible, and we would like to go calmly, like the knight, in dignity, with our friends and family gathered around us to share our sorrow and, perhaps, hope.

HOSPICE

In England, in 1965, Dr. Cecily Saunders started a special treatment center for dying people. She called it *Hospice,* a Latin word meaning "guest"; in medieval times, a stopover station for travelers in the Crusades. Today, a hospice is a stopover for the dying on the way to death. There are two hospice centers in the United States today (in New Haven, Connecticut, and Santa Barbara, California) and hospice programs for home care in thirty-three states.

The hospice atmosphere is comfortable and cheerful, as much like home as possible. Visitors, including children, are encouraged to come often, to talk with the patients (about their death, if they wish), to listen sympathetically, and to try to lessen their fear and loneliness.

Although most people would like to die at home, many families may not be able to cope with this. Death in the past usually came swiftly. Today, with our medical means to keep people alive, death often comes after a long and perhaps painful illness. People with terminal cancer may suffer for months and often need professional care.

Hospice is an alternative to a hospital where doctors and nurses, who want to help people live, may not have time for the dying. In hospitals, drugs are seldom given until pain is severe. In a hospice, drugs are given to prevent pain before it starts. Hospitals are expensive, too. The charge for seventy-six days in a hospital can be as high as $20,000. Whereas hospice care costs $1,000 for the same period.

Hospice tries to make death as positive an experience as is possible. It gives the dying a chance to prepare for death—to plan their funerals, dispose of their possessions, arrange care for their pets—with as little pain and discomfort and as much peace and dignity as possible.

FAMILIARITY WITH DEATH

At one time, every young person had the experience of a death in the family. A century ago, one-third of all the people you knew in your life died by the time you were 12 or 14 years old. Today, you are 65 before this happens! Only 150 years ago, every child had one dead brother or sister.

In those days, people were familiar with death. People died often, and suddenly, of epidemics or disease which struck every age group. Only one child in twenty faces the death of a parent today.

Now that we have learned to control the diseases of infancy and childhood, most people live to an older age. In 1900, two-thirds of the Americans who died were under 50. And, most of them died at home, with their families and friends around them.

Today, death under 50 is considered an early, or *premature,* death. Most of the people who die are over 65 and they die in a hospital or nursing home. Death is far removed from our experience.

THE MEANING OF DEATH

For people who are suffering, death is sometimes a release. When people are in severe pain, or no longer in conscious touch with the world they live in, death may be a relief.

An old woman of southern Italy dies in quiet dignity with members of her family around her, and symbols of her religious faith above her bed.

For people with religious faith, death may mean going to a better world.

Death can also be the occasion for acts of heroism. Soldiers, sailors, police, and firemen sometimes give their lives for their country or to save others. The Spartans stood in the face of death against the Persians at Thermopylae. One thousand Jews at Masada, in A.D. 73, killed themselves rather than surrender to the Romans. Kamikaze pilots in World War II went to certain death on crash-bombing missions.

Through the ages, thoughts of death have inspired great poetry, music, art, and literature, and all the religions of the world.

Death can also be an inspiration to us today.

"I expect to pass through life but once," William Penn wrote. "If therefor, there be any kindness I can show, or any good thing I can do to any fellow being, let me do it now, and not defer or neglect it, as I shall not pass this way again."

Learning about death teaches us the value of life, too.

Each year people die and leave the gift of their words, and thoughts, and deeds to inspire us.

And, each year new young people come into the world: young people who are capable of conceiving fresh ideas that enhance our civilization.

Dying is the natural and necessary end to life.

The knowledge that death will someday come can motivate us to live our lives in such a way that we, too, can form a link in the endless chain of human achievement that stretches from generation to generation.

BIBLIOGRAPHY

Bernstein, Joanne E., and Gullo, Stephen V. *When People Die*. New York: E. P. Dutton, 1977.

Blough, Glenn O. *Discovering Cycles*. New York: McGraw-Hill, 1973.

Cosgrove, Margaret. *Seeds, Embryos, and Sex*. New York: Dodd, Mead, 1970.

Grollman, Earl A., ed. *Explaining Death to Children*. Boston: Beacon Press, 1967.

———. *Talking about Death*. Boston: Beacon Press, 1976.

Klein, Stanley. *The Final Mystery*. Garden City, N.J.: Doubleday, 1974.

Landau, Elaine. *Death: Everyone's Heritage*. New York: Julian Messner, 1976.

Langone, John. *Death Is a Noun*. Boston: Little, Brown, 1972.

LeShan, Eda. *Learning to Say Good-by: When A Parent Dies*. New York: Macmillan, 1976.

Milne, Lorus, and Milne, Margery. *The How and Why of Growing*. New York: Atheneum, 1972.

Pringle, Laurence. *Death Is Natural*. New York: Four Winds Press, 1977.

Segerberg, Osborn, Jr. *Living with Death*. New York: E. P. Dutton, 1976.

Zim, Herbert S., and Bleeker, Sonia. *Life and Death*. New York: William Morrow, 1970.

INDEX